# Explaining
# Biblical
# Meditation

**Campbell McAlpine**

**Sovereign World**

# Explaining Biblical Meditation

**"The life-changing practice of meditating in God's Word."**

**Campbell McAlpine**

Bible quotations are taken from the NKJV
New King James Version. © Copyright 1983
Thomas Nelson Publishers Inc., P.O. Box 141000, Nashville,
TN 37214, USA.


ISBN: 1 85240 158 3


This booklet is abridged from *'The Practice of Biblical Meditation'* (Marshall Pickering)
and *'Alone with God'* (Bethany House Publishers).


SOVEREIGN WORLD LIMITED
P.O. Box 777, Tonbridge, Kent TN11 9XT, England.

Typeset and printed in the UK by Sussex Litho Ltd, Chichester, West Sussex.

# *Contents*

Foreword                                                    7

1   The Importance of Meditation                            9

2   The Companions of Meditation                           13

3   The Blessings of Meditation                            19

4   The Conditions of Meditation – I                       23

5   The Conditions of Meditation – II                      27

6   Meditation – Definition                                33

7   Meditation – Its Product                               39

8   Meditation – Its Practice – I                          47

9   Meditation – Its Practice – II                         53

10  Meditation – Your Beginning                            59

11  Meditation – Your Continuance                          62

12  Meditation – Its Subjects                              65

13  The Final Bugle                                        69

# *Foreword*

As you read this book and apply its truths, I believe it will revolutionise your life. This is not a man-originated assertion or exaggeration, but a God-given promise to those who will meditate day and night in the Word of God:

> *"He shall be like a tree planted by the rivers of water, that brings forth its fruit in its season, whose leaf also shall not wither; and whatever he does shall prosper."* (Psalm 1:3)

The most important words written in this book are scriptures. I encourage the reader to carefully and prayerfully read each one, because it is through God's Word that light comes.

I am indebted to all who have influenced my life to love God and to love His Word. To my parents whose address is heaven; to my wife Shelagh, my constant encourager; to many wonderful friends, and to all whose ministry or writing has enhanced the knowledge of our God and Saviour, Jesus Christ. Greatest thanks of all to Him Who is the 'Word of life' who loved me, and gave Himself for me.

8

# 1

# The Importance of Meditation

The subject of this mini-book is biblical meditation. Of all devotional practices, meditation is probably the most profitable, and yet the most neglected. The results of this approach to God's Word is such, that no earthly wealth could purchase it because the knowledge of God, and His beloved Son Jesus, to quote the Psalmist David, *"is better to me than thousands of coins of gold and silver."* The greatest need in the lives of those who claim to have a relationship with God, is an ever-increasing knowledge of God Himself.

We have moved in to the time predicted by Isaiah the prophet:

*"For behold the darkness shall cover the earth and deep darkness the people; but the Lord will arise over you, and His glory will be seen upon you."* (Isaiah 60:2)

The Church of the living God has to stand, and stand upright, that the power of the Almighty might be manifested through her, and that she might be the light in the darkness that God intended her to be. Daniel reminded us that, *"the people who know their God shall be strong, and carry out great exploits, and those of the people who understand shall instruct many"* (11:32, 33). As never before, it is essential for every Christian to examine his attitude to the Word of God, and the development of this knowledge of God through its contents. At a great price the treasures of the Bible have been given to us over the centuries, and no one has an excuse for ignorance. The knowledge of God is available to all who will give their heart and time to its pursuit. It is the desire of His great heart that we might go on to know Him, and be effective in these 'last days'. Paul encouraged the church at Corinth with these words:

> *"For it is the God who commanded light to shine out of darkness, who has shone in our hearts to give the light of the knowledge of the glory of God in the face of Jesus Christ."*
>
> (2 Corinthians 4:6)

Having shone in our hearts through the light of the 'glorious gospel', we can continually receive more light and more treasure through the knowledge of God and the Lord Jesus.

Have you ever wondered why David knew God so well? He wrote most of the largest book in the Bible, the Psalms. More of David's prayers are recorded than anyone else's, and more of his worship of God than anyone else. He did not possess much of the written Word; he never went to a Bible School or Theological College; he did not have a church to go to; he did not have a library full of commentaries; he did not even have any tapes of wonderful preachers! Where did he get all this knowledge? What was the key? One of the answers to these questions, is that David meditated.

When Joshua took over the awesome task of being leader of the children of Israel from Moses, he must have been scared to death. Wouldn't you have been? However, God spoke to him with encouragement and instruction:

> *"Only be strong and very courageous, that you may observe to do according to all the law which Moses, My servant commanded you; do not turn from it to the right hand or to the left, that you may prosper wherever you go.*
>
> *This Book of the Law shall not depart from your mouth, but you shall **meditate in it** day and night, that you may observe to do according to all that is written in it, for then you will make your way prosperous, and then you will have good success."* (Joshua 1:7, 8)

God gave Joshua a key – 'meditate'. Paul, writing to Timothy also encouraged him to:

10

*"Meditate on these things; give yourself entirely to them, that our progress may be evident to all."*     (1 Timothy 4:15)

Wherever there is the real, there is also the counterfeit. One of the deceits that has ensnared millions, is that true peace and tranquility can be obtained through 'transcendental meditation'. However, the 'mantra' cannot replace revelation by the Holy Spirit. Transcendental meditation seeks to provide a counterfeit practice for men and women who have been created to meditate on God, His character, His words, His works and His ways. Claiming to be non-religious, yet partly Eastern and partly humanistic in its philosophy, it declares that man's questions, and the object of his quest, is within him, and that it is possible for the meditator to arrive at a mental state free from thought, image, and symbol; a state called 'pure being', or 'bliss consciousness', the source of all thought. It fails to acknowledge or deal with man's greatest problem – sin – and therefore eliminates the need for God's answer – a Saviour, Jesus Christ the Lord.

Thank God, we can say 'no' to the counterfeit, and 'yes' to the real. Biblical meditation will revolutionise your life when it becomes a continual part of your devotion, and a consistent feature of your life. As the words of men swirl around you, you will discover that your meditation transforms your own communication, and you will join with the Psalmist in his request:

*"Let the words of my mouth, and the meditation of my heart be acceptable in Your sight, O Lord, my strength and my Redeemer."*                (Psalm 19:14)

**Prayer**

Father, I come to You in the name of the Lord Jesus. I desire to know You better, through Your Word, and by Your Holy Spirit be equipped to know You, and do Your will in these perilous times. Please teach me how to meditate in Your Word, and make it an integral part of my life. I trust You to do this. Amen.

# 2

# The Companions
# of Meditation

It is important when considering a truth from God's Word, to ensure it is interwoven with other truth. The main topic of this book is biblical meditation, which is probably the most rewarding means of obtaining heart-knowledge of God, but the other means must never be neglected.

Let us briefly consider these ways.

## Hearing God's Word

Knowledge is impossible without communication, and God has chosen different ways by which He makes Himself known. One of these ways is listening to God's Word as it is being read, and hearing what God is saying. How many times, in church, instead of intently listening to the Word, we wait to hear what the preacher is going to say about it. Two words are frequently used in scripture, *'hear'* and *'hearken'*. We can hear multitudes of words, and yet hear nothing apart from a sound. However, when we hearken, we give our full attention, and listen carefully, because we believe that what we are hearing is important. It is the Word of God. The message to all the churches in Asia was:

> *"He who has an ear, let him hear what the Spirit says to the churches."*                                            (Revelation 2:7)

Amos prophesied:

> *"Behold the days are coming, says the Lord God, that I will send a famine on the land. Not a famine of bread, nor a*

*thirst for water, but of **hearing** the words of the Lord."*

(Amos 8:11)

He did not say there would be a famine of preaching, or conferences, or church services, but of properly listening to the Word of God. In scripture, hearing is linked with obeying, believing, and receiving His words.

*"But be doers of the word, and not hearers only, deceiving yourselves."* (James 1:22)

## Reading God's Word

Paul wrote to Timothy, *"till I come give attention to reading."* One of the first things a new convert is encouraged to do is to read the Bible. It is explained that when we receive the Lord Jesus into our lives, we have a new Friend. We cannot get to know our new Friend unless He speaks to us, and we speak to Him. Speaking to Him is called prayer, and He speaks to us in a variety of ways, but the main way is through reading His Word. It is obviously important to have a definite, disciplined reading programme, which will take us through the whole Bible. Here are some interesting facts about a normal reader;

- If you read the Bible 15 minutes each day, you will read through the whole Bible in less than a year.

- You could read the whole Bible in 71 hours. The Old Testament would take $52^1/_2$ hours, the New $18^1/_2$.

- If you read by chapters, you could read the whole Bible in 18 weeks by reading 10 chapters a day.

Jesus said;

*"If you abide in My word you are My disciples indeed, and you shall know the truth, and the truth shall make you free."*

(John 8:31, 32)

14

## Studying God's Word

The word 'study' means to exert one's self; to endeavour; to give diligence. It is searching the scriptures, collecting and collating facts on a theme, doctrine, book, character etc., in order to gain a greater knowledge of God. Paul commended the Bereans as those who;

> "...received the word with all readiness, and searched the Scriptures daily to find out whether these things were so."
>
> (Acts 17:11)

Although Solomon wrote, *"much study is a weariness to the flesh,"* there is nothing boring or wearisome in making new discoveries of our great God and Saviour Jesus Christ.

## Memorising God's Word

The children of Israel were continually exhorted to remember;

> "Remember all the commandments of the Lord."
>
> (Numbers 15:39)

> "Remember the words which Moses the servant of the Lord commanded you."
>
> (Joshua 1:13)

Many people claim to have bad memories, but in most cases it is not really a bad memory, but an untrained memory. It is so profitable to store God's Word in our hearts and in our minds. One of the great blessings of meditating in the Word is that so much scripture is also stored in our memories, as we will see in another chapter.

## Singing God's Word

Many of the Psalms are songs. It is wonderful in these days that so much worship in churches includes singing the Word of God.

There is nothing better that we can offer to God, than that which He Himself originated. Singing God's Word also enables us to memorise His Word. Many times in the Psalms we are encouraged to sing;

> *"Sing praise to the Lord, you saints of His, and give thanks at the remembrance of His holy name."* (Psalm 30:4)

> *"Sing to him a new song; play skilfully with a shout of joy."* (Psalm 33:3)

Why not do it now?

## Writing God's Word

Frequently I have been amazed at what I have learned while writing scriptures in times of study or message preparation. Details which have been missed in a reading are often discovered when you write, because you write every word. God through Moses gave clear instruction to future kings;

> *"It shall be when he sits on the throne of his kingdom, that he shall write for himself a copy of this law in a book... and it shall be that he shall read it all the days of his life."* (Deuteronomy 17:18, 19)

## Talking God's Word

What blessing and exhilaration there is in sharing and talking God's Word. Whenever we do this God listens.

> *"Then those who feared the Lord spoke to one another, and the Lord listened and heard them; so a book or remembrance was written before Him, for those who fear the Lord, and who meditate on His name."* (Malachi 3:16)

Keep the recording angel busy!

**Prayer**

Father, thank You for Your Word, and for the various ways by which I can get to know You through it. Help me to discipline my life so that I may do Your will. Please forgive me for every inconsistency in my life, and lack of discipline which has robbed me of the knowledge of You, Your ways and Your will.

Teach me your way, O Lord. I will walk in your truth. Unite my heart to fear Your name. In Jesus' name. Amen.

# 3

# The Blessings of Meditation

*"Blessed is the man who walks not in the counsel of the ungodly, nor stands in the path of sinners, nor sits in the seat of the scornful;*
*But his delight is in the law of the Lord, and in His law he meditates day and night.*
*He shall be like a tree planted by the rivers of water, that brings its fruit in its season, whose leaf also shall not wither; and whatever he does shall prosper."* (Psalm 1:1-3)

It is most interesting how the book of Psalms begins. Right at the beginning we discover the reason why David had such a capacity for God, skill in worship, and knowledge and understanding of the ways of God. He had learned to meditate. Gladly he passes on the blessedness of this devotional practice. These blessings are:

## Happiness

The word 'blessed' means happy, or very happy. It could read, 'O happy man,' or 'O, the happiness of the man.' Our loving heavenly Father not only wants us to be happy, but tells us how to become so. Other scriptures confirm this:

**"Blessed is the man who fears the Lord, who delights greatly in His commandments."** (Psalm 112:1)

**"Blessed are the undefiled in the way, who walk in the law of the Lord."** (Psalm 119:1)

*"Blessed are those who keep His testimonies, who seek Him with the whole heart."*   (Psalm 119:2)

Jesus taught in the 'sermon on the mount' that the way to be blessed or happy was to be poor in spirit; to mourn; to be meek; to hunger and thirst after righteousness; to be merciful and pure in heart; to be peacemakers, and to bless those who persecute you. These are not the recipes of men for happiness, but God's, and included in the Divine recipe is meditation.

## Fruitfulness

Not only does God promise happiness to the meditator, but He also promises fruitfulness. Fruit is the evidence of a right relationship and fellowship with God. It distinguishes between the false and the true. *"You shall know them by their fruits... by their fruits shall you know them"* said Jesus. One morning He left Bethany hungry, and in the distance He saw a fig tree which looked attractive from a distance. However, when He approached the tree He found nothing but leaves – no fruit. A disappointed Jesus said to the tree, *"Let no one eat fruit from you ever again."* If it could not satisfy Him, it could never satisfy any one else. God's people are likened to trees, *"the planting of the Lord."* He comes to us looking for fruit. That evidence of His own life: love, joy, peace. long suffering, kindness, goodness, faithfulness, gentleness and self-control. What a wonderful encouragement to be a meditator, with the guarantee, *"he shall be like a tree... that brings forth its fruit in its season."*

## Freshness

Another promise to the meditator is that he *"shall not wither."* The dictionary meaning of wither is to fade; become dry; to become sapless, and lose vigour. Isn't it refreshing to meet an elderly, or a middle-aged, or a young saint who has never dried up? This morning I had a visit from a friend of mine. When possible we try and meet once a week. I always look forward to his visits because he refreshes me. He is a servant of the Lord, and he loves Him. The two or three hours we spend together is taken up with talking about the Lord, and His Word, and His work. Time flies when we are together, and having spoken **about** the Lord together we then speak **to** the Lord. Although getting older, he hasn't lost his vigour, he hasn't withered... he is a meditator of the Word.

Paul, in writing to Timothy mentioned a friend called Onesiphorus, and said of him, *"he often refreshed me."* Of other friends he said, *"they refreshed my spirit."*

What effect do you have on people? Are you a refresher or a refrigerator? Cheer up! Whatever you are, if you make biblical meditation part of your life, you will never wither, or dry up, but be an encourager of God's people.

## Prosperity

Still another promise to the meditator, *"whatever he does shall prosper."* This must be one of the greatest promises in the Bible for a Christian. Imagine a business consultant approaching the principals of a large corporation and offering them a particular system, which, if adopted would absolutely guarantee profit and success. Man's systems can fail, but God's guarantees are certain. When you become a meditator you can personalise the promise and say, 'whatever I do will prosper.' That is, whatever we do will have the blessing of the Lord on it. The greatest riches in the world are the riches of the knowledge of God and His Son Jesus. It was said of Joseph, *"whatever he did, the Lord made it prosper,"* but that was said of him when he was in prison! In the Bible prosperity is not always linked with material wealth. A Christian can have riches but be a pauper in the knowledge of God, while some who have little of this world's goods are spiritual millionaires because of their knowledge of God, and intimate fellowship with Him. I remember many years ago ministering in Marseilles, in the south of France, and being taken by a friend to visit a Russian couple. We walked through the poor part of the city, then climbed some rickety stairs to a small attic apartment. It was one room, sparsely furnished, and there we met this husband and wife who loved the Lord and were radiant. They sang that great hymn *'How Great Thou Art'* to us in Russian. What a sanctuary that room was. How rich were the occupants. It is not the court that makes the palace, but the presence of the King. We had been with prosperous saints.

There, then, are the blessings which are the result of meditating of God's Word. The blessing of happiness, fruitfulness, freshness, prosperity. There is no greater joy on earth than living with the blessing of God on you. Solomon said:

> *"The blessing of the Lord makes one rich, and He adds no sorrow with it."*                              (Proverbs 10:22)

**Prayer**

Father, thank you for all the blessing You have brought into my life, and thank You for all the blessings You promise me. I do desire to be a fruitful Christian and thank You for choosing me, that I may bring forth fruit, and that fruit might remain. I acknowledge without You I can do nothing, but with You I can do all things. Save me from withering, but help me through Your Word, and by Your Spirit, to be full of Your life, peace and joy. As You offer these wonderful blessings to those who meditate in Your word, continue to teach me how this can be part of my life. In Jesus' Name. Amen.

# 4

# The Conditions of
# Meditation – I

Having reviewed the wonderful promises given to the meditator,
let us now look at the conditions which are necessary for their
fulfilment. This is a simple rule to follow when you read the
Bible. Pay attention to what God says He will do, and also pay
attention to what He tells us to do. If we do what He instructs us,
He will always fulfil His promises... *"if my people will... I will."*

## Separation from sin

The first condition is non-alliance with the ungodly, the sinner,
the scornful;

> *"Blessed is the man who walks not in the counsel of the
> ungodly, nor stands in the path of sinners, nor sits in the seat
> of the scornful."* (Psalm 1:1)

Paul voices the same sentiments;

> *"Do not be unequally yoked together with unbelievers. For
> what fellowship has righteousness with lawlessness? And
> what communion has light with darkness? And what accord
> has Christ with Belial? Or what part has a believer with an
> unbeliever? And what agreement has the temple of God with
> idols? For you are the temple of the living God. As God has
> said, 'I will dwell in them, and walk among them. I will be
> their God, and they shall be My people.' Therefore, 'come out
> from among them, and be separate, says the Lord. Do not
> touch what is unclean, and I will receive you. I will be a*

*Father to you, and you shall be My sons and daughters, says*
*the Lord Almighty.'"* (2 Corinthians 6:14-18)

Although we are called to separation, we are not called to
isolation. Jesus was 'a friend of sinners.' We can have sinner
friends without being involved in their sins, but instead have a
desire to influence them for God; to be sign-posts pointing to the
Lord Jesus. This kind of friendship excludes being emotionally
involved, or having close friendships with those who, as yet, do
not know the saving grace of our Lord Jesus. If we walk in the
counsel of the ungodly, and stand with them in their ways, we
soon will be sitting with them. Included in the prayer of Jesus for
His disciples were these words:

> *"...they are not of the world, just as I am not of the world. I*
> *do not pray that You should take them out of the world, but*
> *that You should keep them from the evil one. They are not of*
> *the world, just as I am not of the world. Sanctify them by*
> *Your truth. Your word is truth."* (John 17:14-17)

The true meditator will be separated from the world. The Word
either separates people from the world, or the world separates
people from the Word. Such separation does not restrict true
happiness, but enhances it. The devil's suggestion to our first
parents in Eden, was that if they obeyed God they would be the
losers, and he is still whispering that lie today. But God says,
*"Blessed is the man"* ...very happy is the man who is separated
from the world. It is good to understand what is meant by 'the
world'. It is not something which is merely external: gambling;
immorality; drunkenness; cheating; etc. Spiritual warfare is not
only against worldly ways, but against the spirit of the world. The
world is unregenerate human nature, whenever or wherever it is
found, either in the church or outside the church. Whether the
world is manifested in distasteful outward form, or in subtle and
refined ways, we must recognise it and repudiate it. James
emphatically writes:

> *"Adulterers and adulteresses! Do you not know that*

24

*friendship with the world is enmity with God? Whoever therefore wants to be a friend of the world makes himself an enemy of God."* (James 4:4)

Choose to be separated **from** sin, and separated **to** God. Choose to love God and not the world. Embrace the cross of our Lord Jesus, and stand with the apostle Paul in total agreement, as he declares:

*"But God forbid that I should boast except in the cross of our Lord Jesus Christ, by whom the world has been crucified to me, and I to the world."* (Galatians 6:14)

Thank God, not only for the saving work of the cross, but also for its separating work. Here is an excerpt from an article written by that twentieth century prophet, the late Dr. A.W. Tozer, entitled, "The Old Cross and the New."

"The old cross would have no truce with the world. For Adam's proud flesh it meant the end of the journey. It carried into effect the sentence imposed by the law of Sinai. The new cross is not opposed to the human race, rather it is a friendly pal, and if understood aright, it is the source of oceans of good clean fun, and innocent enjoyment. It lets Adam live without interference. His life motivation is unchanged, he still lives for his own pleasure, only now he takes delight in singing choruses and watching religious films, instead of singing bawdy songs, and drinking hard liquor. The accent is still on enjoyment, though the fun is now on a higher plane morally, if not intellectually.

The new cross encourages a new and entirely different evangelical approach. The evangelist does not demand abnegation of the old life, before the new life can be received. He seeks to key in to public interest, by showing that Christianity makes no unpleasant demands, rather it offers the same thing the world does, only on a higher level. The new cross does not slay the sinner. Rather it redirects him. The old cross is a symbol of death. It stands for the abrupt and violent end of a human being. The man in Roman times who took up His cross and started down the road had already said farewell to His friends. He was not coming back. The cross made no compromise, modified nothing, it slew all of the man, completely and for good. It struck cruel and hard, and when it had finished its work, the man was no more. The race of Adam is under death sentence. There is no commutation, and no escape... our message is not a compromise, but an ultimatum."

What are the results of such separation? Friendship with God; peace; true happiness; intimate fellowship. *"I will be a Father to you, and you shall be My sons and daughters, says the Lord Almighty."*

**Prayer**

Father, I want to glory in the cross of the Lord Jesus. I acknowledge it separates me from the world. I choose this separation. Please give me a continual love for those who do not know You, and let my life and witness speak of You. I do not want to walk in the counsel of the ungodly, or stand in the way of sinners, or sit in the seat of the scornful, and I thank You that You are able to keep me from evil, and evil influences. I want to know the fear of God which is to hate evil, keeping me free from love for the world. Please reveal Yourself to me through Your Word, and let it have such an abiding place in my life, that I will be clean through the words You speak to me, as Jesus promised. Amen.

# 5

# The Conditions of Meditation – II

The second essential the Psalmist gives to the meditator is to *"delight in the law of the Lord."* To delight simply means to take pleasure. This will be an increasing experience as you meditate, as new discoveries are made in the Word of the wonders of God and His ways. David is speaking out of the depth of his personal experience, and there is abundant evidence in the Psalms, that to him, God's Word gave him absolute joy. Several of these pleasurable outbursts are found in Psalm 119:

*"I will delight myself in Your commandments which I love."*
(v.47)

*"Your testimonies also are my delight..."* (v.24)

*"The law of Your mouth is better to me than thousands of coins of gold and silver."* (v.72)

*"How sweet are Your words to my taste, sweeter than honey to my mouth."* (v.103)

*"Your word is very pure, therefore Your servant loves it."*
(v.140)

*"I rejoice at Your word as one who finds great treasure."*
(v.162)

David certainly did not find God's Word dry, dull or boring. Why? We can find two main reasons which we will now consider.

## Delighting in the Lord

One cannot delight in the Word without delighting in the author. As it was with David, so it should be with us. He loved God. God was his pleasure, his joy, his life. He determined it would be so, and so it was. He said, *"I will love You, O Lord."* One of the principal ways of showing our love for God, and our delight in Him, is to discover and fulfil the things that give Him pleasure. Here are some of these things:

● Loving those who love God
*"I love those who love Me, and those who seek Me diligently will find Me."* (Proverbs 8:17)

● Obeying God
Jesus said, *"He who has my commandments and keeps them, it is he who loves Me. And he who loves Me will be loved by My Father, and I will love him and manifest Myself to him."* (John 14:21)

● Following after righteousness
Solomon wrote, *"The way of the wicked is an abomination to the Lord, but He loves him who follows righteousness."* (Proverbs 15:9)

● Serving God in the right way
Paul wrote, *"For the kingdom of God is not eating and drinking; but righteousness and peace and joy in the Holy Spirit. For he who serves Christ in these things is acceptable to God and he who serves Christ in these things is acceptable to God and approved by men."* (Romans 14:17, 18)

Joyless service gives God no pleasure. God said of Israel, *"you did not serve the Lord your God with joy and gladness of heart, for the abundance of everything."* (Deuteronomy 28:47)

● Giving cheerfully to God
Giving is like serving, both should be done with joy. Paul wrote to the Corinthians, *"let each one give as he purposes in his heart, not grudgingly, or of necessity; for God loves a cheerful giver."* (2 Corinthians 9:7)

John McNeil, a Scottish minister was once preaching on this verse, and described a cheerful giver as a man in church who shouted, 'Hallelujah, here comes the collection plate!'

● Praying with a right heart

How God loves to hear us, and what delight He receives when we pray with a sincere, believing heart. *"The prayer of the upright is His delight."* (Proverbs 15:8)

● Praising God with a right heart

How good David was at this. He said, *"I will praise the name of God with a song, and I will magnify Him with thanksgiving. This also shall please the Lord better than an ox or bull, which has horns and hooves."* (Psalm 69:30, 31)

● A broken and a contrite heart

Multitudes have been blessed and comforted by the humility, brokenness, and confessions of David after his adultery with Bathsheba, and after ordering the death of her husband, Uriah. God hates sin, but He is merciful to the truly repentant. Like the prodigal's father, He delights to see the wanderer coming back home. David said, *"For you do not desire sacrifice, or else I would give it; You do not delight in burnt offering. The sacrifices of God are a broken spirit. A broken and a contrite heart – these O God, You will not despise."* (Psalm 51:16, 17)

● Seeking to please God in everything

Giving pleasure and delight to God can be summed up in the words of Paul:

> *"For this reason we also, since the day we heard it, do not cease to pray for you, and to ask that you may be filled with the knowledge of His will in all wisdom and spiritual understanding. That you may walk worthy of the Lord, **fully pleasing him,** being fruitful in every good work and increasing in the knowledge of God. Strengthened with all might, according to His glorious power, for all patience and long-suffering with joy."* (Colossians 1:9-11)

## Delighting in the Will of God

The natural sequence of delighting in the Lord will be delighting in His will. David said, *"I delight to do Your will, O my God, and Your law is within my heart"* (Psalm 40:8). The will of God is not meant to be a mere obligation, but a pleasure. How important it is to be convinced that the will of God is not just something which is good, but something which is best. There is no real joy, lasting peace, or fulfilment for the child of God, outside His will. We should therefore yield ourselves totally to Him, both to know and to do His bidding. As a matter of fact, we cannot truly know His will, unless we are surrendered to it, as Paul explained to the Christians in Rome, when he wrote:

> *"I beseech you, therefore, brethren, by the mercies of God that you present your bodies a living sacrifice, holy, acceptable to God, which is our reasonable service. And do not be conformed to this world, but be transformed by the renewing of your mind, that you may prove what is that good, and acceptable, and perfect will of God."*        (Romans 12:1, 2)

Choosing to do the will of God is essential for the meditator. Jesus said, *"If anyone wills to do His will, he shall know concerning the doctrine, whether it is from God, or whether I speak on My own authority."* (John 7:17)

Submission to God will cause a free flow of revelation through the Word, as we borrow the words of the Lord Jesus to make them our own desire, *"I do not seek My own will, but the will of the Father Who sent Me."* (John 5:30)


## Delighting in His Word

When the Lord, and doing His will, is our delight, then we will delight in His Word. This pleasure will increase as we continue to hear His voice and increase in the knowledge of Him. Meditation is not a technical exercise, but a loving relationship in which He communes with us and we with Him.

30

## Application

Be still before the Lord now. Tell Him you want to delight in Him and in His will and His Word. Ponder some of the things that please Him, and make them applicable in your life:

● Loving those who love God
Is there someone you do not love? Some resentment, bitterness, something unforgiven? Confess it to the Lord, and pray God's blessing on that person or persons.

● Obeying God
He has promised to manifest Himself to those who obey Him. Is there any disobedience in your life? Chose to be obedient and thus give Him joy.

● Following after righteousness
Tell Him you choose to do the right thing, to be honest and upright in all your dealings with God, and with men.

● Giving
Choose to please the Lord by giving to Him generously and cheerfully, as an expression of your love for Him.

● Praying and praising
How wonderful that today we can please Him by our praying and praising. Not only does He hear us, but He delights to hear us.

● Delighting to do His will
Yield yourself completely to Him by presenting your body. When He has our body He has everything, because housed within us is our soul and spirit. Now take the words of David, and make them yours. *"I delight to do Your will, O my God."*


## Prayer

My Father, I come to You in the name of the Lord Jesus, realising that without You I can do nothing. I want to give You pleasure and joy, by delighting in You, Your will, and Your Word. Here is my body which I present to You. It is not mine in any case, because it has been bought by the precious blood of Jesus. I acknowledge that, and only give what is rightfully Yours. Please help me by the power of Your Spirit, to love what You love, and hate what You hate. Save me from a joyless service, and powerless life. Help me to love all who love You; to be obedient to all that You tell me; to live uprightly and to give cheerfully. May my prayers and praise be acceptable in Your sight.

Thank You for all the revelation of Yourself that I am going to receive through Your Word as I learn to meditate in it. I want Your word to be the voice of my Beloved to my heart; the comfort and guidance of my Good Shepherd, the loving instruction from my perfect Teacher; light from You who are the Light of the world; truth from You whom I acknowledge as *the way, the truth and the life.*

You are so gloriously and majestically delightful, and I thank and praise and worship You. Amen.

# 6

# Meditation – Definition

Let us now consider what meditation is, and seek to define it.

## The Inner reception of Truth

Meditation is the devotional practice of pondering the words of a verse, or verses of scripture, with a receptive heart, allowing the Holy Spirit to take the written word and apply it as living word in to our inner being. The result is the impartation of Divine truth, bringing a response to God. Someone has described meditation as 'the digestive faculty of the soul'. Jeremiah wrote:

> *"Your words were found and I **ate** them, and Your word was to me the joy and rejoicing of my heart."*　(Jeremiah 15:16)

Meditation is inwardly receiving the Word of God, illustrated by eating or feeding. God spoke to Ezekiel;

> *"You shall speak My words to them, whether they hear or whether they refuse, for they are rebellious. But you son of man, hear what I say to you. Do not be rebellious like that rebellious house; open your mouth and **eat** what I give you. Now when I looked, there was a hand stretched out to me; and behold a scroll of a book was in it. Then He spread it before me; and there was writing on the inside and on the outside, and written on it were lamentations and mourning and woe. Moreover He said to me, 'Son of man, **eat** what you find; **eat** this scroll and go, speak to the house of Israel.' So I opened my mouth, and He caused me to **eat** that scroll.*

33

*And He said to me, 'Son of man, **feed** your belly, and fill your stomach with this scroll that I give you.' So I **ate**, and it was in my mouth like honey in sweetness."*

(Ezekiel 1:7-10, 3:1-3)

## More Truth – More Life

Jesus made this wonderful statement:

*"It is the Spirit who gives life; the flesh profits nothing. The words that I speak to you are spirit and they are life."*

(John 6:63)

Therefore the more of the Word we inwardly receive, the more life we receive. This is one of the basic principles for spiritual growth. His words are living words; they are spirit and life words, and as they are imparted to us, our spiritual capacity is increased. It is so important to understand this vital truth. Let us look at another scripture. Peter is teaching the importance of the knowledge of God, and says this of God's Word:

*"His divine power has given us all things that pertain to life and godliness, through the knowledge of Him who called us by glory and virtue. By which have been given to us exceeding great and precious promises, that through these you may be partakers of the divine nature, having escaped the corruption that is in the world through lust."*

(2 Peter 1:3, 4)

In other words, Peter is saying that when you believe a promise of God, you receive something of God Himself, something of His divine nature. Let me illustrate. Supposing you came to faith in Jesus Christ in a church service. The Holy Spirit convicted you of your sin, and you heard the great news that God loves you and that Jesus died for you. Now somewhere there came to you *"an exceeding great and precious promise."* It may have been John 3:36; *"He who believes in the Son has everlasting life."*

34

What happened when this Word was believed and inwardly received? You were given everlasting life. Now everlasting life is something of the divine nature. You received something of God Himself. There is a promise I like to take to the Lord every morning, because every morning I am a candidate;

*"If any of you lacks wisdom, let him ask of God who gives to all liberally, and without reproach, and it will be given to him."*                                                    (James 1:5)

What happens when this promise is believed and inwardly received? In admitting to God that my human wisdom is insufficient to do the will of God, to make the right decisions, to cope with the various and unexpected circumstances of every-day living, and asking Him for His wisdom, He imparts His wisdom to me. Now wisdom is part of the divine nature, so the more I receive of Him, and from Him, the more I grow, and the more I grow, the more of His life will be manifested through me. Through meditation there is a continual impartation of His Word, His truth, His life.


## More Truth – More Light

Not only is there life in truth, but there is also light. David said:

*"The entrance of Your words gives light. It gives understanding to the simple."*                                               (Psalm 119:130)

Therefore the more of the Word of God we inwardly receive, the more light we receive. Notice that David said, *"the entrance of Your words."* Not merely looking at truth, or admiring truth, but inwardly receiving it. In Exodus 16 we read of God's provision of manna for the children of Israel. Here was 'bread from heaven' to feed and sustain them. What did people do when they saw it? Did they admire it, analyse it or dissect it? No, they **ate** it, and inwardly received it. This is what happens in true meditation, and as we receive more truth, more of the Word, we also receive more light. Jesus said, *"You are the light of the world,"* and we shall shine brighter and brighter as we allow His Word to enter our hearts. That same Word will illuminate our way and be *"a lamp to our feet, and a light to our path."*

## Revelation

Meditation is receiving revelation through His Word. All truth which vitally affects our lives, and changes them, does not come merely by explanation, but by revelation. Most of us can remember truths we have read, or heard ministered, and we believed they were true because they were in the Bible, but there was no heart understanding. Then one day we said, 'Now I see it.' What happened? Did we have an increase in our I.Q? No, we received revelation, and that truth became meaningful and personal in our lives.

Many times verses of scripture are like flowers which have closed their petals because the sun has gone down. You look at the flower and admire it because it is part of God's creative miracle, but there is much beauty you cannot see. In the morning when the sun rises, the flower begins to open up towards the light, and then you can see the full beauty and colours, and details. In the same way we can look at scripture and know it is good because of the author, and yet fail to behold the beauty and detail it contains. However, when you meditate, dependent on divine illumination by the Sun of righteousness, there comes revelation and insight, giving you an increased knowledge of the Creator, and an impartation of knowledge, of which you now become a steward. This reminds us of how dependent we are on the Holy Spirit to give us such revelation. Paul reminds us:

> *"Eye has not seen, nor ear heard, nor have entered into the heart of man, the things which God has prepared for those who love Him. But God has revealed them to us through His Spirit. For the Spirit searches all things, yes the deep things of God. For what man knows the things of man except the spirit of the man which is in him? Even so no one knows the things*

*of God except the Spirit of God."*     (1 Corinthians 2:9-11)

Jesus promised the disciples that when the Spirit of truth came, He would guide us into all truth. How wonderful to have the greatest Teacher in us, and with us, to reveal truth to us.

## Summary

Meditation is the practice of pondering, considering, and reflecting on verses of scripture, in total dependence on the Holy Spirit to give revelation of truth and meaning, and by obedient response and reception of that Word, having it imparted to our inner being. The impartation of such truth brings life and light to the meditator, as a result of an attitude of humility, trust and obedience.

Meditation is inwardly receiving truth. It is feeding on Christ, who is the Living Bread and Living Word. The word 'meditate' is taken from the Latin root word, medicalus, from which we get the word medicine. Medicine in the bottle has no effect. It has to be received internally – normally three times a day!

## Prayer

Father, thank You that by Your grace and mercy I am a son of God, and a child of the King. I thank You that You delight to reveal Yourself through Your Word. I come to You, childlike, depending on You completely to give me revelation, which I desire to receive and obey. Let Your Word indeed be a lamp to my feet, and a light to my path. Amen.

# 7

# Meditation –
# Its Product

The Word of God is a treasure which produces great riches in and
from the lives of those who meditate in it. In the King James
version, one can read the letter the translators wrote to the King,
when they submitted the new version to him;

> "But among all our joys, there was no one that more filled
> our hearts, than the blessed continuance of the preaching of
> God's sacred Word among us; which is that inestimable
> treasure, which excelleth all the riches of earth; because the
> fruit thereof extendeth itself, not only to the time spent in
> this transitory world, but directeth and disposeth men unto
> that eternal happiness which is above in heaven."

How true, as we receive the Word it does 'extend itself' because
it is life, and produces life, and that life is manifested in the one
who has chosen to be a *"doer of the Word, and not a hearer only."*

**The Fear of the Lord and the Knowledge of God**

It is obvious that David, having known the blessedness of
meditating on God's Word, passed on to his son Solomon this
treasure. Solomon gives such a clear definition of meditation, and
its results:

> *"My son, if you receive my words, And treasure my commands
> within you, So that you incline your ear to wisdom, and
> apply your heart to understanding; Yes, if you cry out for
> discernment, and lift up your voice for understanding, If you*

*seek her as silver, and search for her as for hidden treasures;*
*Then you will understand the **fear of the Lord** and find the*
***knowledge of God.***"                                (Proverbs 2:1-5)

The greatest product of meditation is the fear of the Lord,
and the knowledge of God. The fear of the Lord is the
beginning of wisdom, and the beginning of knowledge.
Solomon reminds us that the way to have this knowledge is
to receive the word; treasure it; have it within you; seek and
search.

## Meditation brings a respect for God's ways

David said;

*"I will meditate on Your precepts, and contemplate Your*
*ways. I will delight myself in Your statutes; I will not forget*
*Your word."*                                (Psalm 119:15, 16)

As he pondered and considered the commands and directions
of God in meditation, it caused him to give them his full respect,
with the result of joyous obedience.

## Meditation strengthens us to resist temptation

David received much opposition in his life both from enemies
without, and enemies within. He was the object of criticism and
judgement, yet he testifies that meditation prevented him from
wrong reactions. He says:

*"Princes also sit and speak against me, but*
*Your servant meditates on Your statutes."*        (Psalm 119:23)

The more the Word of God is in us, the better equipped we are to
resist sinning. The word 'statute' means, 'within a decreed limit.'
The decreed limit for the child of God is the will of God. We get to

know the will of God through the Word of God. David did not retaliate by defending himself, or attacking his opponents, but he reacted according to the Word of God which was within him.

## Meditation produces an increased love for the Word

The more we eat and taste of the Word of God, the larger our appetites and love for it becomes. When you eat the best, it causes you to lose taste for that which is inferior. Isaiah wrote:

> *"Butter and honey He shall eat, that He may know to refuse the evil, and choose the good."* (Isaiah 7:15)

David's meditation in the Word and obedience to it, produced an ever-increasing love for God, and for what He said. He expresses this:

> *"I will delight myself in your commandments which I love. My hands also I will lift up to your commandments which I love, and I will meditate on Your statutes."*
> (Psalm 119:47, 48)

> *"Oh, how I love Your law! It is my meditation all the day."*
> (Psalm 119:97)

This too will be your experience as a meditator.

## Meditation gives understanding

Again we quote David:

> *"I have more understanding than all my teachers, for your testimonies are meditation. I understand more than the ancients, because I keep your precepts."* (Psalm 119:99, 100)

He did not say he had more knowledge than his teachers, but

he did have more understanding. What is the use of knowledge if you do not understand it? Mere knowledge, Paul reminds us. *"puffs up."* There are three words which are often used by Solomon in the Book of Proverbs; knowledge, understanding, and wisdom. Knowledge is being acquainted with the facts. Understanding is having insight as to what the facts mean. Wisdom is the ability to apply what we know and understand to our lives and circumstances. David's testimony to meditation was that it gave him understanding.


## Meditation always brings a response to God

This is such an important product of meditation. All real meditation will bring a response to God. That response may be confession, praise, thanksgiving, worship, prayer or intercession, but there *will always be a response to God.*

Now here is a wonderful thing. By meditation we will receive more, but God will also receive more from us. You will always know that your meditation has been completed, because in some way you have responded to God.

There is a testimony given by a great saint called George Muller. In the early 1830s, he was challenged by the faithlessness of so many of his contemporaries, and longed, in his words, for 'visible proof' that God our Father is the same faithful God as ever He was. God directed him to initiate a programme to house and care for orphans in the city of Bristol, England. He looked to God and God alone, to supply every need, and the story is a vibrant testimony to the faithfulness of God. He testified to the great blessing meditation brought to his life:

> "It has pleased the Lord to teach me a truth, the benefit of which I have not lost for fourteen years. I saw more clearly than ever, that the first business to which I ought to attend every day, was to have my soul happy in the Lord. The first thing to be concerned about was not how much I might serve the Lord, but how I might get my soul in a happy state, and how my inner man might be nourished. I might seek truth to

42

set before the unconverted, I might seek to benefit believers, I might seek to relieve the distressed, and I might in other ways seek to behave myself as it becomes a child of God in this world, and yet, not being happy in the Lord, and not being strengthened in the inner man day by day, all this might not be attended to in the right spirit.

Before this time my practice had been to give myself to prayer after having dressed in the morning. Now I saw the most important thing I had to do was to give myself to the reading of the Word of God and to meditate on it, thus my heart might be comforted, encouraged, warned, reproved, instructed, and that thus, by means of the Word of God, my heart might be brought into experimental communion with the Lord.

I began therefore to meditate on the New Testament from the beginning, early in the morning. The first thing I did after having asked in a few words the Lord's blessing upon His Word, was to begin to meditate on the Word, searching as it were every verse to get a blessing out of it... not for the sake of public ministry, nor preaching, but for obtaining food for my soul.

The result I found to be inevitably this. After a few minutes my soul had been led to confession, or thanksgiving, or intercession, or supplication, yet it turned almost immediately to prayer. When thus, I had for a while been making confession, or intercession or supplication, or having given thanks, I go to the next words of the verse, turning all as I go into prayer for myself or others, as the Word may lead to it, but still continually keeping before me that food for my own soul is the object of my meditation.

The difference, then, between my present practice and my former is this. Formerly when I arose, I began to pray as soon as possible, and generally spent all my time till breakfast in prayer, or almost all the time. At all events I almost always began with prayer, except when I felt my soul to be more than usually barren, in which case I would read the word. But what was the result? I often spent a quarter of an hour, or half an hour, or even an hour on my knees before having been conscious to myself of having derived comfort, encouragement, humbling of the soul etc., and often after having suffered much from wandering thoughts, for up to half an hour, I only then began to really pray. I scarcely ever suffer in this way now, for my heart, being brought into experimental fellowship with God, I speak to my Father about the things He has brought to me in His precious Word. It often astonishes me that I did not sooner see this point."

George Muller proved that meditation was a life changing devotional practice, always bringing a response from God.

## Meditation day and night

Another product of meditation, is that what God has said to us, does not disappear but keeps returning. David was not shut away in some cloister. He was a busy king, father, husband, soldier, statesman. God also told Joshua to meditate, 'day and night' and he too, was busy. Meditation has sometimes been illustrated by a cow chewing the cud. I had used this in teaching, but once while I was ministering in a Bible School in Switzerland I went for a walk in the country, and came to a field with cows in it, and with their bells tied around their necks. I stopped to study them, and learned some lessons. Firstly I noticed they only chewed the cud when they were resting. Obviously there would have been no cud unless they first had eaten, but what they had eaten kept coming back. They would chew a bit more on it, swallow, and soon it would come back again. So it is with meditation. You can meditate in a verse in the morning, and during the day or night it keeps coming back when you can 'chew' on it a bit more!! In another place I saw a cow chewing the cud while its calf was feeding from its mother. Another lesson! Our ability to feed others is dependent on what we ourselves have received.

No doubt David learned to meditate when he was a shepherd, spending days and nights out in the open fields, and contemplating the wonders of God and His creation. He said:

> *"My eyes are awake through the night watches, that I may meditate on Your word."*　　　　　　　(Psalm 119:148)

What an encouragement to meditate. It produces the fear of the Lord and the knowledge of God; it causes us to respect the ways of God; it strengthens us to resist temptation; it produces an increased love for God and His Word; it gives us understanding; it brings forth response to God; it keeps coming back.


**Prayer**

Father, I want to continue to thank You for the treasure-house of Your Word, containing truth and revelation that no wealth on earth could buy. I want to be a diligent seeker of truth, not only receiving knowledge, but also understanding. Thank You that Your Word will cause me to respect Your ways, and walk in them. Strengthen me to resist temptation; help me not to react to the flesh. I praise You that my love for You and Your Word will increase, and like David, I will delight myself in Your commandments, and incline my heart to Your ways. Amen.

# 8

# Meditation – Its Practice – I

Having considered the importance, blessing, conditions, definition, and product of meditation, we now come to its practice – the 'how to'. The story in Luke's gospel of Jesus, after His resurrection, meeting up with the two disciples on the Emmaus road, illustrates certain truths which need to be applied as we practice meditation.

## Sitting with the Lord

When the Lord accepted the invitation into their home, it is recorded that He *"sat at meat with them."* This is the first requirement; to sit relaxed before the Lord. This obviously does not mean that we can only meditate when sitting, but indicates the importance of our attitude of restful waiting on Him. We may have been busy with so many things, and have many things on our minds, but now we come to meet with Him and hear His voice, through His Word. We need to put aside all distracting thoughts, and pray as Wesley did:

> Expand Thy wings celestial dove,
> Brood o'er our natures night,
> On our disordered spirits move,
> And let there now be light.

Solomon said, *"I sat down in his shade with great delight, and his fruit was sweet to my taste."* (Song of Solomon 2:3). Before Jesus fed the multitude He commanded them first to sit down. We need to ensure that our hearts are right with Him, with no unconfessed sin, coming with restful confidence in the knowledge that as we draw near to Him, He draws near to us.

## Hearing the voice of God

How important it is to know and recognise His voice. Impressions come from four main sources;

- Other people.
- Ourselves.
- The devil.
- God.

While meditating you are usually on your own, so are uninfluenced by other people. Because we want His thoughts, and not our own, it is important to deal with our thoughts, as we prepare to hear from God. How can we do this?

## Impressions from ourselves

Proverbs 3:5, 6 tells us:

> *"Trust in the Lord with all your heart, and lean not on your own understanding. In all your ways acknowledge Him, and He shall direct your paths."*

Bring this as a prayer to God, with a sincere heart, and tell Him you come trusting Him to speak to you through the Word, and that you are not depending on your own understanding or intellect, because *"he who trusts in his own heart is a fool."* (Proverbs 28:26)

Tell Him that you do acknowledge Him in all your ways, and trust Him to direct your paths; and thank Him that you are going to hear His voice. We are totally dependent on Him and His Holy Spirit, to help us to receive His thoughts.

**Impressions from the devil**

We do have an enemy, but he has been defeated by our blessed Lord Jesus. However, we are not ignorant of his devices. He does not want Christians to be strong in God, through the knowledge of God. But there is protection from any inroads he would seek to make, and we can stand against him in the name of the Lord Jesus. Arm yourself with these scriptures, and use them with faith, whenever you are conscious of his attacks or his diversions, and also as your protection;

> *"Therefore submit to God. Resist the devil and he will flee from you."* (James 4:7)

> *"You are of God, little children, and have overcome them, because He who is **in** you is greater than he who is in the world."* (1 John 4:4)

> *"And they overcame him by the blood of the Lamb and by the word of their testimony, and they did not love their lives to the death."* (Revelation 12:11)

> *"Therefore humble yourselves under the mighty hand of God, that He may exalt you in due time. Casting all your care upon Him, for He cares for you. Be sober, be vigilant; because your adversary the devil walks about like a roaring lion, seeking whom he may devour. Resist him, steadfast in the faith, knowing that the same sufferings are experienced by your brotherhood in the world."* (1 Peter 5:6-9)

> *"Put on the whole armour of God, that you may be able to stand against the wiles of the devil... Stand therefore, having girded your waist with truth, having put on the breastplate of righteousness, and having shod your feet with the preparation of the gospel of peace. Above all taking the shield of faith with which you will be able to quench all the fiery darts of the wicked one. And take the helmet of salvation, and the sword of the Spirit, which is the word of*

*God. Praying always with all prayer and supplication in the Spirit, being watchful to this end with all perseverance and supplication for all saints."* (Ephesians 6:11, 14-18)

When we come against the enemy, submitted to God, and in the name of the Lord Jesus, resisting the devil, then he **must** flee, and we will therefore not receive any impressions from him. Praise God for His victory, and that in Him we can be continual overcomers.

## Impressions from God

Having dealt with the other sources of impression, we now trust the Lord to speak to us through His Word, and know that He will. All that He says will glorify His name, causing us to worship Him. It will always agree with the Word of God, and will impart knowledge of Himself. It will not cause us to be *"puffed up"* with knowledge, but will enable us to love Him and others more. What He says will be true, honest, just, pure, lovely, and of good report. It will be the voice of the good Shepherd which we, His sheep, will recognise, and follow. His Word will be *"the joy and rejoicing"* of our heart, because we have come to Him saying, *"speak Lord, for Your servant hears"* knowing that we will never be disappointed. We will go from our time of meditation with a sense of awe and wonder because we have heard the voice of the Almighty. His Word will linger, and return, because it has been imparted to us, becoming part of the very fibre of our being, bringing life and light, and the knowledge of the Holy.

## Christ the Giver

The Emmaus story confirms we are completely dependent on the Lord to feed us from His Word. As the disciples sat at the table with Jesus, **He** took the bread, **He** blessed it, **He** broke it, and **He** gave it. They sat and received it. So it is in meditation. We read a verse or verses, ponder it, consider it, but He is the One who gives revelation and understanding. Meditation is not an intellectual exercise, although God does not bypass our minds. It is not puzzling over what the scripture means, nor is it delving into some commentary to get another's thoughts, (good as this may be), but it is allowing the Master to impart to us personally from His loving heart.

The result was that *"their eyes were opened and they knew Him."* They received, not merely a revelation of truth, but a revelation of Christ. Although He disappeared out of their sight, the wonder and joy remained, and with burning hearts they rushed to Jerusalem to share with others what they had received from Him.

### Application

Consider the various points of this chapter, and then make them a matter of prayer:

**Sitting with the Lord.** Some find this easier than others because of their temperament. Some have a placid disposition, and others a restless one, but both need the help of the Lord. Share with the Lord any difficulties you have in this realm, and tell Him what specific help you need. Why not write them down?

_____

_____

_____

_____

_____

_____

**Hearing God's voice.** Have you had difficulty here? Tell the Lord about it, and apply the teaching of this chapter, looking to Him and not *"leaning to your own understanding."* Take God's protection against the enemy. Use the Word of God against him, submit yourself to God, stand, resist, and take the place of victory in Jesus.

**Looking to Jesus.** Acknowledge that He is *"the giver of every good and perfect gift"*. He is the One who takes the Word, blesses it, breaks it and gives to you. Ask Him to help you to receive it.

### Prayer

Father, open my eyes that I may see wonderful things out of Your Word. Teach me to rest in You, and hear Your voice. Thank You that because Christ is in me, and I am in Him, I can resist all the power of the enemy. Feed me from Your word, that I may know You. Thank You. Amen.

# 9

# Meditation –
# Its Practice – II

Having seen the necessity of a restful, but attentive attitude towards the Lord; the dealing with our own thoughts, and resisting any work of the enemy, we now proceed to answer some important questions to enable us to start to meditate.

### Where should I meditate?

Because God knows us so well, our needs and our situations, it is important to ask Him. In doing this we are again, *"acknowledging Him in our ways."* Sometimes in the reading of the Word a verse or verses are quickened to us, and we have a desire to meditate on them, so that we may receive all that God wishes to reveal, and that is good. However, because God is a God of order, and He has compiled the Bible in a special way, it is most strongly recommended that the best method of meditation is a systematic, verse by verse meditation. The first step is to ask God to put in to our minds the book in the Bible in which He wants us to meditate, then starting at chapter one, verse one, proceed through the whole of that book. It may take six months or a year, to complete meditating through a particular book. So that you may start right, discover now where God wants you to meditate. We are going to put into practice the teaching of the previous chapter, by asking God to put into your mind the book in the Bible in which He wants you to meditate. Ready? Tell the Lord you die to your own thoughts and choice of books, and you only want His will. Now pray your own prayer, or follow this one;

"Father, I come to You as Your child, having chosen to be a

meditator of Your Word each day. I surrender my own choice, and ask You now to put into my mind the book in which you want me to meditate. Thank You. Amen."

Be still… the first book that comes to your mind is His answer. Now write down the book He has given you.

The Lord has shown me to meditate in _____

_____

Date _____

Well done. When you have completed that book, then ask the Lord what the next one should be. Don't forget the promises to the meditator. Blessed, fruitful, prosperous.


## How long should I meditate?

The answer to this question is, meditate until you have received from the Lord. Initially it is advised to set aside at least fifteen minutes. Remember that the Word we receive will continually return to our minds, like the cow chewing the cud!! The Lord can give revelation of truth in a few minutes or it may take longer. He knows our schedules, and He is always a rewarder of those who diligently seek Him. There is little progress in Christian living without the discipline of time with God.


## When is the best time to meditate?

One cannot to dogmatic or legalistic in answering this question. The best time is when you can sit down unhurriedly with the Lord. A mother with a young child will not find much time until about mid-morning. People on shift-work will have to adapt according to their work programme. However, because we have chosen to *"seek first the kingdom of God and His righteousness,"* meditation is going to have a priority in our lives, together with the other means of approaching the Word. There is no doubt, that where it is possible, first thing in the morning is the best time possible. Some feel more relaxed in the evening, but as someone has said, 'why tune up the fiddle when the concert is over?'

Determine what is the best time for you, and discipline your life accordingly.


## What should I do when I am not sure whether the thoughts are mine, or His?

Sometimes this question may come to your mind. A simple way to deal with it is to ask the Lord that if it is not from Him to remove it, and if it is from Him to confirm it. He is such a wonderful teacher and friend, and He will respond to our requests when He sees we really want to know Him and do His will. When doubts arise, certain questions can be asked to test whether it is of God, such as:

Does it glorify God, and exalt the Lord Jesus?

Is it edifying?

Does it increase my knowledge of Him, and His ways?

Is it in harmony with the rest of scripture?

Does it bring a response to God of prayer, praise, thanksgiving, worship, or confession?

Remember the words of the Lord Jesus;

*"If anyone wills to do His will, he shall know concerning the doctrine, whether it is from God or whether I speak on My own authority."* (John 7:17)

As long as we choose to do the will of God, He will not allow us to go outside it.

## What do I do if I am getting nothing from the verse?

If you ever experience a 'dry period', and there seems to be no revelation, speak to the Lord about it. He loves honesty, and we can tell Him exactly how we feel, and what the situation is. There are obvious questions we should ask;

Have I obeyed what He has told me to do previously?

Did I expect God to speak to me?

Am I leaning on my own understanding?

Am I relying on the Holy Spirit to lead me in to all truth?

If these questions do not reveal anything wrong, rest in Him, and if nothing is coming from that verse, move on to the next.


## All true meditation will bring a response to God

Without apology we repeat this vital truth about meditation; there is always a response to God. God communes with us, and we with Him. Part of meditation is praying scripture. That great saint of the seventeenth century, Mme Jeanne Guyon, whose writings greatly influenced such people as John Wesley, and Jesse Penn Lewis, encouraged people to 'pray the scriptures.' She said that praying scripture was not judged by how much was read, but by the way it was read. She said that reading quickly was like a bee skimming the surface of a flower, but praying the scripture was like the bee penetrating deep into the depths of the flower to remove the deepest nectar.

In the Psalms we see how David's meditation brought a variety of responses to God;

| Meditation | Response |
|---|---|
| *"My heart was not within me; while I was musing, the fire* | Prayer *"then I spoke with my tongue,* |

*burned."*

*Lord, make me to know my end and what is the measure of my days, that I may know how frail I am."*     (Psalm 39:3, 4)

*"When I remember You on my bed, I meditate on You in the night watches."*

Praise
*"my mouth shall praise You with joyful lips."*   (Psalm 63:5)

*"I remember the days of old; I meditate on all your works; I muse on the work of your hands."*

Expressed longing for God
*"I spread out my hands to You; my soul longs for You like a thirsty land."* (Psalm 143:5, 6)

Other scriptures: Psalm 49:3; 77:12; 104:34; 119:48.

## Can I include study with meditation?

Sometimes while meditating there is a desire to know more about the meaning of a particular word or subject, which the verse may suggest. There is nothing wrong with gaining more knowledge through a concordance, commentary, or dictionary. However, having gained that knowledge, bring it back to the verse and include it in your meditation.

## How can I retain what I receive in meditation?

In meditation the Holy Spirit takes the Word and imparts it within us. That Word becomes part of us when it has been received. The Holy Spirit also brings truth to our remembrance when needed. Jesus gave this great promise to His disciples;

*"But the Helper, the Holy Spirit, whom the Father will send in My name, He will teach you all things and bring to your remembrance all things that I said to you."*     (John 14:26)

# 10

## Meditation – Your Beginning

This is the day you can now start as a meditator, putting into practice the things you have been learning. You are going to learn as you do it. Ready?

### Wait on the Lord

Be still... Is everything all right between you and the Lord? Spend a minute or two thanking Him for His goodness and grace to you. Praise Him for Who He is. Worship Him. Pour out your love to Him. Yield yourself totally to Him, trusting Him to give your His thoughts.

Open your Bible at the book God gave you, at chapter one. If you have not already done so, read through the first chapter, so that you have a knowledge of the context. Now go to verse one, and read the verse word by word slowly. Then reread it with an open heart and mind to receive His thoughts from it.

As an aid in starting, write out the first one or two verses.

_____

_____

_____

_____

_____

_____

_____

_____

_____

Now write the thoughts you have received.

_____

_____

_____

_____

_____

_____

_____

Now write what your response was to God.

_____

_____

_____

_____

_____

_____

**Summary**

What did I learn about God today?

_____

_____

What did I learn about myself?

_____

_____

_____

What did I praise Him for?

_____

_____

_____

What, and who did I pray or intercede for?

_____

_____

_____

Finish by worshipping the Lord.

Choose to recall your meditation throughout the day and night, and you will find the Lord will keep giving you more, as well as establishing what you have received.

Well done – Praise the Lord.

# 11

## **Meditation – Your Continuance**

This is your second day. Remember what the Lord said to you yesterday? It has remained, hasn't it?

It is not suggested that you write out your meditation and responses every day, unless you wish to, but the purpose of doing it again is to help you, and encourage you in the early days.

Date_____ Book _____ Chapter 1, verse ____

Write out the verse you are meditating on today.

_____

_____

_____

_____

_____

_____

Your meditation.

_____

_____

_____

_____

_____

_____

_____

_____

_____

Your response.

_____

_____

_____

_____

_____

_____

As you finish by praising the Lord, tell Him you are available to share with others what He has shared with you, if He opens the way for this, and you sense it is His will. People like 'fresh bread'.

Also, make yourself available to teach someone else how to meditate. Once you have done it yourself you are qualified to teach someone else. Introduce your wife, husband, children, or friends to this rewarding way of getting to know God.

Borrow David's prayer:

> _"Let the words of my mouth, and the meditation of my heart, be acceptable in Your sight, O Lord, my strength and my Redeemer."_ (Psalm 19:14)

or this prayer poem:

My God, I thank You for Your Word,
That comes like medicine or a sword,
To change my life that I may be
In greater likeness unto Thee.

Speak how You will, that is Your choice,
In thunders peal or still small voice,
Your Word is truth, Your Word is light,
To show me how to live aright.

Reveal Yourself that is my plea,
Reveal Yourself O God to me,
Show me your will, show me Your ways,
That I may serve You all my days.

*'Let there be light'* You once did cry,
And brilliant radiance filled the sky,
Command again that light to me,
That I may more Your glory see.

You Living Word, I praise Your Name,
Your are forever more the same,
You spoke to prophet, priest and king,
Then speak to me, Your Word to bring.

I thirst for You, My God, My Lord,
And open up Your sacred Word,
I come to drink, I come to feed,
Then meet my very deepest need.

Come Holy Ghost, come heavenly dove,
Show me my Lord, the One I love,
And speak to me that I may say,
Yes… God spoke to me today.

Give me Lord Your revelation,
Through Your word in meditation,
And let it ever to me bring,
The knowledge of my Lord and King.

Campbell McAlpine

# 12

# Meditation –
# Its Subjects

There are several themes upon which we can meditate, as we discover in the life of David.

## The Word of God

Most of this booklet has been devoted to meditating in God's Word, so we will not add anything.

## On God and His Son, Jesus Christ

There are many times when we can meditate on God, and on the Lord Jesus. We can do this in the silence of waiting on Him, contemplating His greatness, pondering all the glorious facets of His perfect character; remembering His faithfulness; reflecting on His glory, grace, goodness, holiness, justice, longsuffering, love, mercy, power, wisdom, justice, judgements, knowledge, gentleness. What will be the result? There will be response. We will be lost in 'wonder, love and praise' as the hymn writer put it. Worship will rise to our God for all that He is, and all that He has done, and all that He has promised to do. We can meditate on His names. We can meditate on the cross, and pour out our thanksgiving for His amazing grace. We can ponder the glory and power of His resurrection; His ascension; His position at the right hand of God. We can contemplate His coming again.

David said:

*"My meditation of Him shall be sweet; I will be glad in*

*the Lord."* (Psalm 104:34)

*"My soul shall be satisfied as with marrow and fatness, and my mouth shall praise You with joyful lips, when I remember You on my bed. I meditate on You in the night watches."*

(Psalm 63:5, 6)

## The work of God

*"I will remember the works of the Lord; surely
I will remember Your wonders of old.
I will also meditate on all Your work, and talk of your deeds."*

(Psalm 77:11, 12)

Remembering all the works that God has done in the past is not only an incentive to praise, but a stimulus to faith. Many times in scripture the writers deliberately bring to remembrance the works of God. *"Remember His marvellous works that He has done; His wonders, and the judgements of His mouth"* cries David in Psalm 105:5. Many of the Psalms are taken up with the mighty things that God has done in history, to encourage us to trust Him for the present and for the future. Just prior to his death, Moses gathered the children of Israel together, and to encourage them in their taking possession of the Promised land, recounted the mighty things that God had done in delivering them from Egypt, and providing for them in the wilderness. You, too, can remember the things God has done for you, as well as others in the past. As the old hymn says, 'Count your many blessings name them one by one, and it will surprise you what the Lord has done.' Meditate on the work of God.

## The works of God's hands

Not only did the Psalmist meditate on the work of God, but also on the works of God's hands;

*"I must muse* (meditate) *on the work of your hands."*

(Psalm 143:5)

God spoke to many of His servants through His creation and His creatures. Before God gave Abraham the promise of the multiplication of his seed, He told him to contemplate the works of His hands, the stars:

*"Then He brought him outside and said, 'Look now toward heaven, and count the stars if you are able to number them.' And He said to him, 'so shall your descendants be.'"*

(Genesis 15:5)

If we have eyes to see, there is so much which declares His greatness, and causes us to worship and praise Him.

*"The heavens declare the glory of God; and the firmament shows His handiwork."* (Psalm 19:1)

We are asked to consider one of the smallest works of His hands, and learn from it;

*"Go to the ant, you sluggard! Consider her ways and be wise. Which having no captain, overseer, or ruler. Provides her supplies in the summer, and gathers her food in the harvest."* (Proverbs 6:6-8)

Yes, God speaks in so many ways and teaches so many lessons, from a corn of wheat; seed that falls into the ground; trees; a rock; the grass; the lily of the field; the thunder and lightening; rain; dew; a spring of water; a mustard seed; a watered garden; etc. There is so much to meditate on of the works of His hands.

I was once teaching biblical meditation at a Bible school in Hawaii. After mentioning the practice of meditating on the works of God's hands, I took the class outside, and told them to go and sit down somewhere, and in reliance on the Lord, meditate on some work, or works of His hands, allowing God to speak to them. They did so for over an hour, and then we gathered back together again to share what God had said. It was staggering to hear the many things God had revealed, and the lessons which had been learned during that time. The God who *"at various times and in various ways spoke in time past to the fathers"* still speaks today in such a variety of ways. Meditation quickens our senses to be perceptive to what He is saying, either in the Word, while meditating on Himself, or His work, or the works of His hands. May our attitude always be, *"Speak Lord for Your servant is listening,"* – and expect an answer.

## Prayer

Yes, Lord, please help me to be perceptive, and alert to any way, or to any means you choose to speak to me. Give me eyes to see, and ears to hear. Amen.

# 13

## The
## Final Bugle

The call to meditate is not a polite evangelical request to adapt a useful technique that will brighten up the 'quiet time.' Rather is is a command to be disciplined; to think clearly; to be prepared; to be watchful, and above all to know God and His Son Jesus Christ. We should consider it as a clear instruction from God which deserves our attention and obedience:

*"You shall meditate in it day and night."* (Joshua 1:8)

*"Set your hearts on all the words which I testify among you today."* (Deuteronomy 32:46)

*"Ponder the path of your feet."* (Proverbs 4:26)

*"Consider your ways."* (Haggai 1:7)

*"Let these words sink down into your ears."* (Luke 9:44)

We are living in days of gross darkness. The effects of evil are going to become more evident in our society. The church will be purified, and there will be a separation of true from false, real from counterfeit. Much of Paul's writings in the epistles is directed by an awareness of the perilous circumstances of those to whom he wrote. As year succeeds year, it seems that our circumstances as believers, in the society in which we now live, places us in the same context as Paul's readers. As I write, I reflect on what has happened even in recent weeks; earthquakes; floods; fires; nation warring against nation; increase in crime and violence, with politicians impotent in dealing with such disorder.

The Church has been too often characterized as an institution that is constantly sitting down at cross-denominational, cross this and cross that discussion, meeting or conference: the irony being that the impact and demands of the Cross of Christ have not surfaced through the agenda.

The call to meditate is a call to heed the words of God, because only His words minister life; release light; illuminate our thinking on the greatest matters we can know – the mighty character of God, and His purposes for our lives, the Church, the world, and for eternity.

There is a great need in our day to be sharpened, and to be more urgent in the way we approach the things of God. Assurance has so often led to a kind of self-contented smugness that has strangled spiritual life. In many areas 'movements' have led to the cultivation of their own gardens, which bloom unmindful of the spiritual foliation that has been wrecked by the havoc of the war of darkness against the souls of men. To meditate is to be continually exposed to the work of the Holy Spirit, who through the Word of God, will lead us from self-examination to an examination of the world in which we live. As we observe with the eyes of God, we will be mobilised to give our lives even as God was moved to give His only begotten Son. We will not overcome with church models, or our corporate personality. The abiding Word of God is the means of overcoming the wicked one.

We must repent of our sloth in our dealings with God's Word. The 'fruit salad' of religious ideas is served with doctrinal 'casseroles', and we are content with a state of affairs in the church of the living God which would not be tolerated in a school of business. The command to meditate, coming with urgency from the heart of God, is a call to think His thoughts, and to learn of Him. How will you fare in the battle which wages for the minds of men, without the mind of God? We must mentally develop. Meditation will leave you in no doubt that the Christian mind has a wholly supernatural orientation, and will convince you that it is only as the Word of God abides in you, that you will survive the violent collision between the mind of Christ and earthly culture. It is the life of Christ in us that will remain unshaken.

I mention again in closing what I said at the beginning of this book. If you become a meditator in God's Word, without any exaggeration it will revolutionise your life. This is not a man-originated assertion, but a God-given promise.

> *"He shall be like a tree, planted by the rivers of water, that brings forth fruit in its season, whose leaf also shall not wither, and whatever he does shall prosper."* (Psalm 1:3)

It will require discipline and perseverance. The more you know God the greater menace you are to the kingdom of darkness, therefore opposition can be expected, but there is victorious power in the name of **Jesus**. There is no greater knowledge on earth than the knowledge of the God of heaven. The importance of this was declared by the prophet Jeremiah:

> *"Thus says the Lord. let not the wise man glory in his wisdom. Let not the mighty man glory in his might, nor let the rich man glory in his riches; But let him who glories glory in this, that he understands and knows Me, that I am the Lord, exercising loving kindness, judgement, and righteousness in the earth. For in these things I delight says the Lord."*
>
> (Jeremiah 9:23, 24)

and a closing word from Daniel:

> *"The people who know their God shall be strong, and carry out great exploits, and those of the people who understand shall instruct many..."* (Daniel 11:32, 33)

If you have enjoyed this book and would like to help us to send a copy of it and many other titles to needy pastors in the **Third World**, please write for further information or send your gift to:

**Sovereign World Trust, P.O. Box 777, Tonbridge, Kent TN11 9XT, United Kingdom**

or to the **'Sovereign World'** distributor in your country. If sending money from outside the United Kingdom, please send an International Money Order or Foreign Bank Draft in STERLING, drawn on a **UK** bank to **Sovereign World Trust**.